SCHIRMER'S LIBRARY
OF MUSICAL CLASSICS

Vol. 1883

David Popper

High School of Cello Playing
(40 Etudes)

Op. 73

G. SCHIRMER, Inc.

DISTRIBUTED BY

HAL•LEONARD®
CORPORATION
7777 W. BLUEMOUND RD. P.O. BOX 13819 MILWAUKEE, WI 53213

Printed in U.S.A.

High School of Cello Playing
(40 Etudes)

No. 1

David Popper, Op. 73
(1843-1913)

Allegro molto moderato.

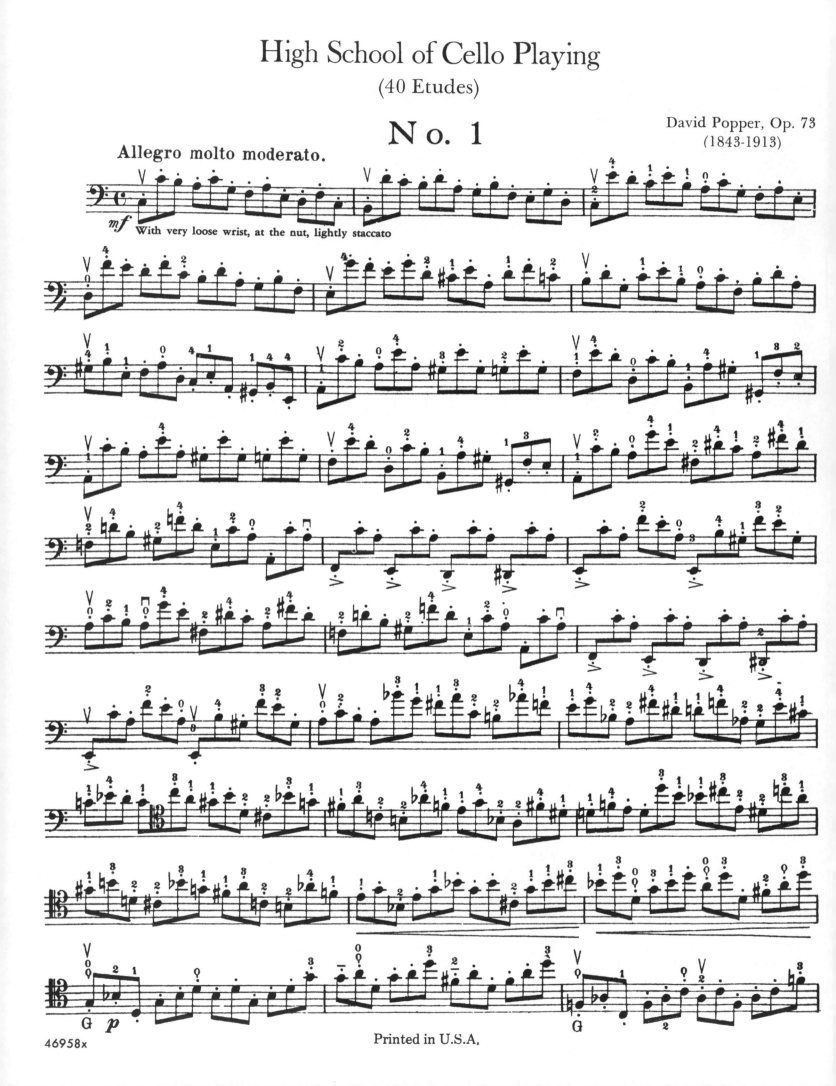

mf With very loose wrist, at the nut, lightly staccato

Printed in U.S.A.

No. 2

No. 3

No. 4

Andante con moto.

No. 5

Allegro non troppo.

No. 6

No. 7

gently sliding

46958

No. 8

Andante.

This Study has to be executed throughout with very steady bow and light, scarcely perceptible bend of the wrist, in passing over from one string to another.

No. 9

Andante sostenuto.

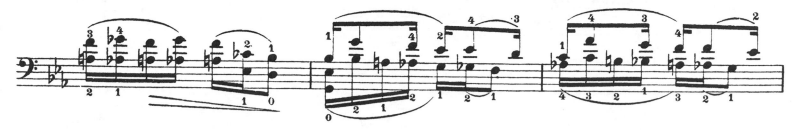

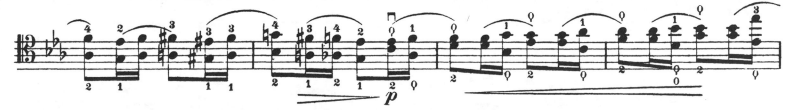

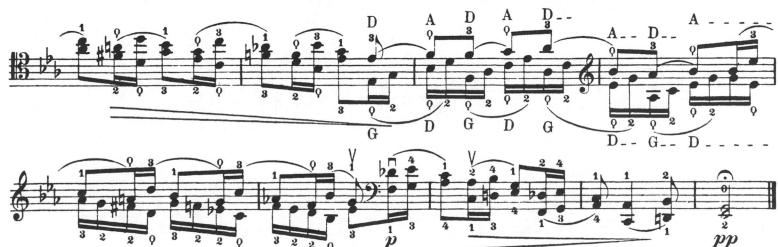

No. 10

Appassionato.

46958

No. 11

Moderato

No. 12

Allegro.

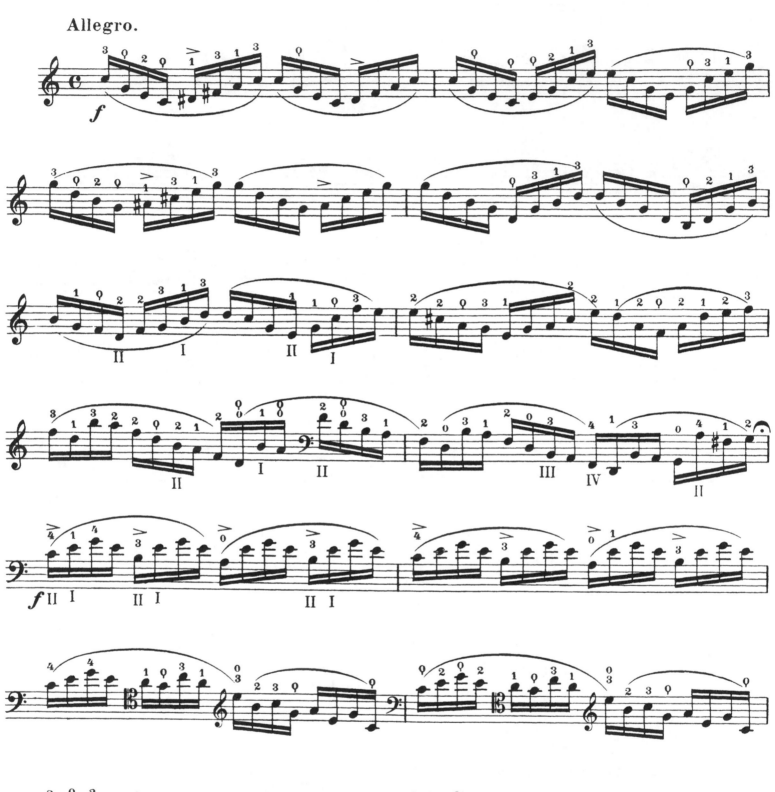

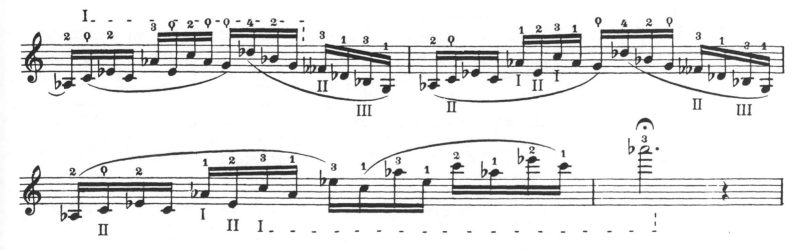

No. 13

Allegro molto moderato.

No. 14
(Study in Staccato)

31

No. 15

Allegro.
Scherzando.

No. 16

Allegro moderato.

p (capriccioso)

No. 17

No. 18

Allegro molto moderato.

Very light with the bow

No. 19
*)("Lohengrin" Study)

Allegro.

*) The first measure only of this Study has been taken from a Violoncello passage in the 3rd Act of "Lohengrin," which the cellists generally find somewhat difficult, especially in the tempo prescribed.

No. 20

Appassionato.
Allegro.

No. 21

Allegro molto moderato.

No. 22

No. 23

Moderato.

No. 24

Allegro moderato.

51

46958

No. 25

Allegro assai.

To be played nearest to the point of the bow.

No. 26

Andante con moto.

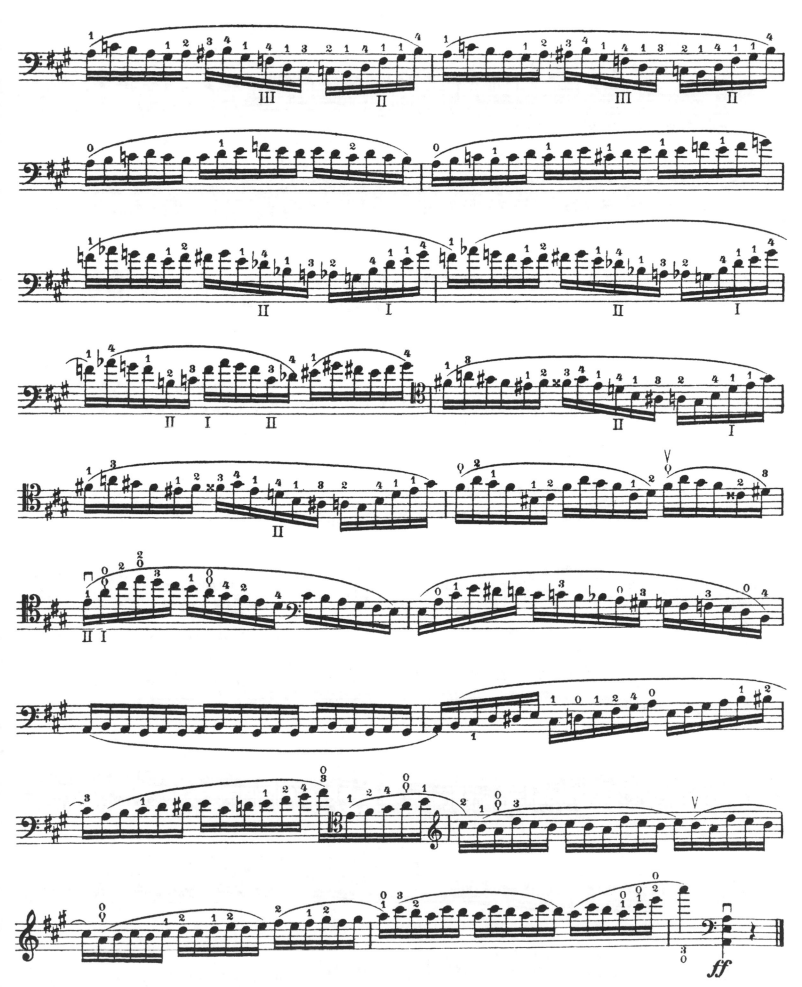

No. 27

Allegro.

mf To be played throughout with springing bow.

No. 28

Andantino grazioso.

*) The first note of each sextuplet to be emphasized slightly and melodically.

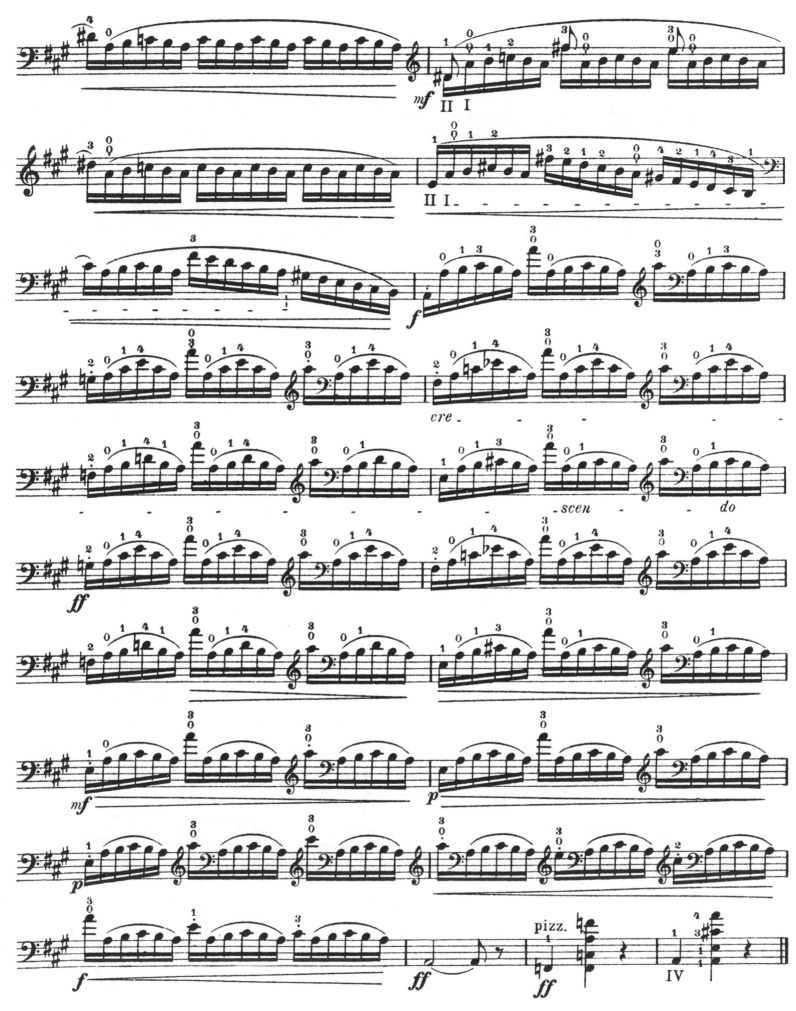

No. 29

No. 30

No. 31

No. 32

No. 33

lightly at the point

No. 34

Andante espressivo.

No. 35

No. 36

No. 37
(Study in Mordents)

No. 38

No. 39

85

46958

No. 40
(Study in Harmonics)